# *Exploring*
# VIETNAM

Dr. Diana Prince

AuthorHouse™
1663 Liberty Drive
Bloomington, IN 47403
www.authorhouse.com
Phone: 833-262-8899

Because of the dynamic nature of the Internet, any web addresses or links contained in this book may have changed
since publication and may no longer be valid. The views expressed in this work are solely those of the author and do not
necessarily reflect the views of the publisher, and the publisher hereby disclaims any responsibility for them.

All photographs are the sole property of the author.

This book is printed on acid-free paper.

ISBN: 979-8-8230-3949-9 (sc)
ISBN: 979-8-8230-4284-0 (hc)
ISBN: 979-8-8230-3950-5 (e)

Library of Congress Control Number: 2024926110

Print information available on the last page.

Published by AuthorHouse  01/22/2025

authorHOUSE®

# *Exploring*

# Vietnam

# Introduction

Exploring Vietnam is a photographic journey of a significant country in our recent past. In this book, over a hundred photographs will document a country in conflict during this century, and the significant impact it has had on the world we know today.

This book will deal with three aspects of Vietnam:

*Halong Bay and the Vietnam Coast*

*People and Places of Vietnam*

*Vestiges of the Vietnam War*

## HALONG BAY AND THE VIETNAM COAST

Halong Bay and the Vietnam Coast are spectacular in their beauty. Rugged, forested slopes rise from the turquoise waters, creating a magnificent panorama of shapes and sizes. Halong Bay has 1,600 islands, and it is a world-heritage site.

Many of these imposing peaks, rising from the sea, tower over even the largest vessels cruising in the still waters.

In some places, dragon boats, with their brilliant colors, ply the still waters against the background of the gigantic peaks that soar high above them. The shining waters mirror this otherworldly landscape. The towering peaks are striking creations of nature over the centuries. On the outskirts of the spectacular waterfront, tourist boats ply the waters. Local fishing abounds and sightseeing boats operate for the tourists who come here.

Many generations of local families have also made this place home. Their modest but colorful houseboats cluster around a network of small local offshore piers, which are essential for the local families, as well as for visiting fishermen. Even the youngest children use small boats to navigate in their villages, and for transport to their nearby schools.

**PEOPLE AND PLACES OF VIETNAM**

Despite decades of war and challenges, the Vietnamese people are friendly and welcoming to newcomers. Visitors will find their interactions genuine and enthusiastic.

One unique experience is a visit to the Mekong Delta. Here long slender boats navigate the narrow waterways, among lush palms and a heavily forested landscape. Long slender boats carry newcomers on hidden waterways. Protected by native-made straw hats, the long boats glide through waterways alive with windblown palms and water birds.

In great contrast to the river regions, the streets of Hanoi are bustling and alive with tourists. Merchants sell everything from popsicles on the street, to classy attire in upscale shops. Street vendors set up their fresh trove of fruits and vegetables. The vendors are friendly and welcoming.

In the heat of the day, people gravitate to the many small parks and city ponds—well-kept and peaceful hideaways in the midst of a large city.

Children are everywhere—friendly and as fascinated with visitors as the visitors are with them.

Small shrines are not unusual in city parks or even adjacent to some houses. Motorcycles are popular and especially maneuverable in the cities, where car traffic is usually heavy.

Hanoi is especially interesting, from its fine museums featuring antiquities, to its ultra-modern hotels such as the Caravelle Hotel.

In Ho Chi Minh City, formerly known as Saigon, the Notre Dame Cathedral features a large statue of the Virgin Mary on a pedestal in front of the Church. It is a city landmark.

In Da Nang, the International Airport is a modern landmark, among the other nearby streets mixing older sections of the city with newer enclaves of building.

Small parks abound, with pagodas and stone stairways. On the outskirts of town, local villages have small shrines outdoors to commemorate their departed family members.

On the outskirts of the city are small rural communities, with some small farms.

**VESTIGES OF THE VIETNAM WAR**

Hanoi had been a colonial city occupied by the French for nearly half a century. The country regained its independence in August of 1945.

The country of Vietnam began on September 2, 1945. At that time, Ho Chi Minh of the Communist party seized power. The new country was officially called the "Democratic Republic of Vietnam".

A decade later, in 1955, the country became engaged in a war which was to decimate much of the country with bitter fighting. The unrest endured for two decades with a significant impact and loss of life. Politics, the difficult terrain, and the swamps and jungles made the combat challenging and difficult.

North Vietnam was allied with the Soviet Union, North Korea and China.

South Vietnam was allied with the United States, Australia, New Zealand, the Philippines and Thailand.

America's involvement ended when the Paris Peace Accord was signed.

Hanoi is the capital of Vietnam. The name means "between two rivers", and it is situated between the Red River and the Black River. It is the capital of culture and politics. Hanoi had been the country's capital for nearly a thousand years.

In 1964, after two destroyers of the United States were fired upon in the Gulf of Tonkin by the North Vietnamese, President Lyndon Johnson increased United

States military activity in the region. This directly involved the United States in the Vietnam War.

After the confrontation in the Gulf of Tonkin, President Lyndon Johnson sent troops to the region. Despite superior weaponry of the United States, and its allies, there were unexpected confrontations and losses.

Two factors made the fight experience difficult. First, guerrilla tactics such as booby traps and extensive underground tunnels, were employed. This challenged the Americans' conventional weapons and means of warfare. The Americans also confronted dense forests and unfamiliar war tactics, as well as difficulties maneuvering in some dense and formidable territory.

One of the great obstacles was the underground Cu Chi Tunnel System which extended over 250 miles, and was used by the Viet Cong in the Vietnamese War. This was a complex underground tunnel system on the outskirts of the city of Saigon. Maneuvering within the close confines of the tunnels was difficult. Some soldiers referred to themselves as "tunnel rats."

The extensive underground network of tunnels was a defense against the United States and Allied forces. This elaborate underground tunnel system was equipped with kitchens, sleeping quarters, kitchens and even underground classrooms. The elaborate system was a maze of secret entrances, trap doors and hidden hatches. The longest was four miles in length and extended to Da Nang and to Hue in central Vietnam.

This elaborate underground tunnel system extended all the way to the border with Cambodia. The still existing portion is located west of Saigon near Cu Chi. It is now open for tourists to enter and explore. Over 1,200 Americans from the Vietnam War are still unaccounted for. Over 42,000 soldiers died during the Vietnam War.

Today, Vietnam is a surprisingly diverse country which includes Taoism, Confucianism and Buddhism. There is also a significant Catholic population. An enduring practice in Vietnamese homes is an altar built to honor the ancestors of their family.

# CHAPTER ONE

## *Halong Bay and the Vietnam Coast*

View from the Vietnamese Coast

Morning in Halong Bay

Early Morning View from Mast Head

Water Reflections in Halong Bay

Starting Out

View from the Shore

Forested Coast of Vietnam

Morning Fog Rolling into the Bay

Heading Out to Sea

Morning Dawns in Halong Bay

Dragon Boat Onshore

Young Boat Captain

17

Dragon Boat Figurehead

Light Across Halong Bay

"Split Rock" Island Across the Bay

Small Boat Dwarfed by Lofty Island Peak

Charting a Direction

Tourist Boat Setting Out

Tourists Waiting on the Docks

Preparing for the Journey

Morning at the River

Working on the Docks

27

Tourist Boat in Halong Bay

Fishing vessels head out to sea in the early morning.

Children Out for an Early Morning Ride

Family Pets Relax on the Family Dock

Transporting Food by Boat

Early Morning Onshore

Tourist Boats are Popular

Morning Laundry Drying in the Sun

Boats Heading out to Sea in the Early Morning

Morning Laundry Drying on the Docks in the Sun

Trees Line the Vietnamese Coastline

A Chinese Junk plies the waters off the rugged Vietnamese Coast.

Onshore boats provide tourist rides as well as fishing opportunities.

Bikers Take an Early Morning Break

Morning at the Beach

Early Morning in Vietnam

Beach Umbrellas Waiting for Tourists

Beach Vessels Waiting for Fishing and Recreation

Visitors Cross the Narrow Bridge to the Island

Early Morning Near the Dock

# CHAPTER TWO

## *People and Places*

Mekong Delta Early Morning Ride

Mekong Delta on the River

Navigating a Boat at the Mekong Delta

Tourist Restaurant over Lush Green Vegetation

Cruising Down the Mekong River

Morning in Hanoi

Early Morning in a Hanoi Park

Local Children in Hanoi

Selling Vegetables in Hanoi

A Shrine Near Hanoi to Honor a Goddess

City Park Near Hanoi

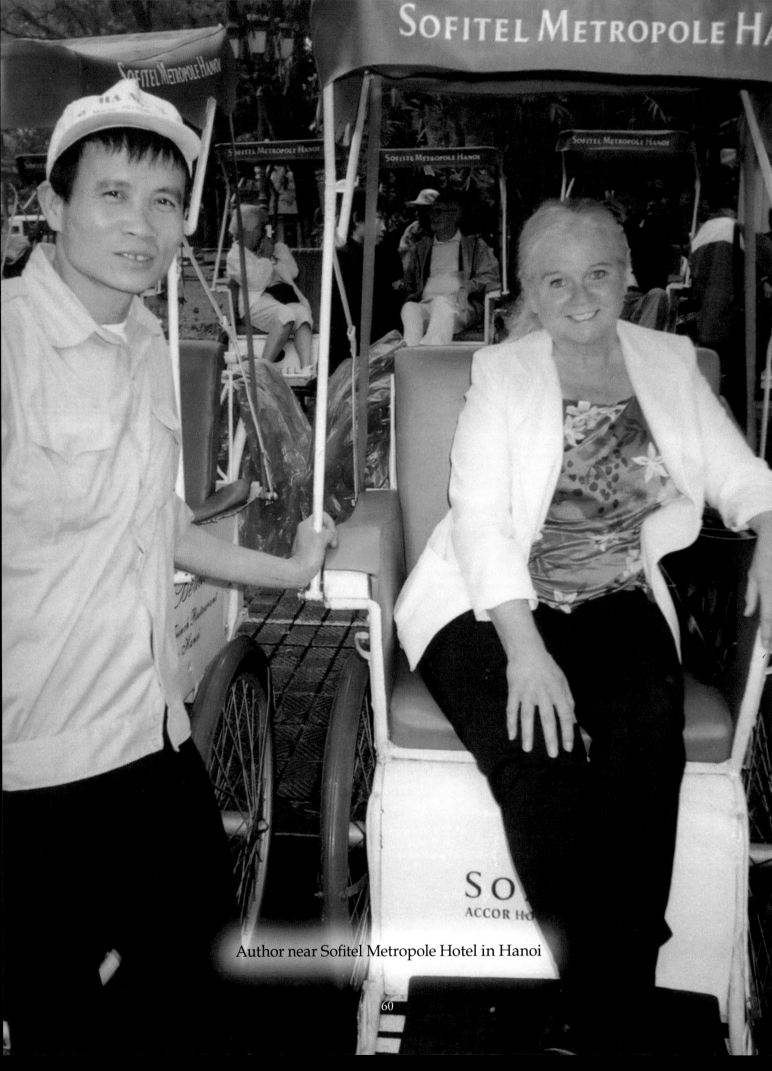

Author near Sofitel Metropole Hotel in Hanoi

Flower Shop in Hanoi

Caravelle Hotel at Hanoi

Overlooking Vietnamese Park near Hanoi

Large Statue of the Virgin Mary in front of the Notre Dame Cathedral in Ho Chi Minh City

64

Airport at Danang

Water Garden in Danang

School Near DaNang

Stonecutter Shop in Danang

Pagoda in City Park at Danang

Pond in City Park near Danang

Rural Village

# CHAPTER THREE

## *Vestiges of the Vietnam War*

Wall Fortification from the Vietnam War

Thick Jungle Bush Concealing Entrance to Underground Cu Chi Tunnels

War Fortifications with Barbed Wire

American War Plane on Display in Vietnam

American Tank from the Vietnam War

American Fighter Jet on Exhibit from the Vietnam War

Visitors at the War Plane Exhibit of American Aircraft from Vietnam War

Battlements and Old Barracks

Battlement Relic at Fort

Two Statues with Weapons and Uniforms Dating to the Vietnam War Period

HỒ BOM B.52
B.52 BOMB CRATER

Concealed Entrance Way to Underground Bunker

Crumbling Battlement Walls

Extensive Camouflaged Bunkers Lie Under this Area

One of the entrances to the underground tunnels
at the Cu Chi Tunnels near Hanoi.

Entryway into One of the Cu Chi Tunnels

Man Stands in Entryway into One of the Cu Chi Tunnels

Young man is sitting at one of the entrances to the Cu Chi Tunnels

Demonstrating Entry into the Cu Chi Tunnels

Young Man Demonstrating One of the Very Small
Entry Points into the Cu Chi Tunnels

For Tourist purposes in recent years, the openings to some of the tunnels were
enlarged for tourists to more easily enter and explore the underground tunnels.

This shows the current entryway to one of the Underground Tunnels.

This shows the narrow stairs into the Cu Chi underground tunnel system.

This shows some Tourists Climbing Down the narrow, steep steps into the Cu Chi Tunnel System.

This photo shows the enlarged dug-out entry that leads into the first room of this underground tunnel.

This photo shows where some underground munitions
were stored in the Cu Chi Tunnels.

This photo is taken in the narrow Cu Chi Tunnel system where part of the underground path opens up into a large, natural underground cave.

This area was a bedroom in an underground passageway of the Cu Chi Tunnel.

Leaves and debris litter the floor of the Cu Chi Tunnel. It has a low ceiling which makes it difficult to navigate. In some places a person must crawl through, instead of standing up.

This part of the Tunnel has been "booby-trapped". Note that in the leaves and debris littered on the floor of the Cu Chi Tunnel, sharp and dangerous spikes have been deliberately installed, rising sharply from the floor. These were meant to deter any one who entered, especially in darkness. Because this part of the tunnel has a low ceiling, it makes it difficult to navigate. These sharp pointed spikes would have seriously injured anyone trying to walk through or crawl through this space.

This opening to the sky can be seen from deep inside the Cu Chi Tunnels. In
some cases, supplies could be lowered down through this opening by ropes.
In other cases, a soldier could be lowered down or hoisted up
out of the cave in an emergency through this opening.
The entry point was also closely guarded against detection by
the enemy, who could have also entered into the underground
tunnels by this opening, and attempted a surprise attack.

This abandoned room of the Cu Chi Tunnel is open to the sky. The sky can be seen day and night from this vantage point. In some cases, supplies could be lowered down through this opening by ropes. In other cases, a fighter could be lifted down or hoisted up out of the cave in an emergency through this opening. The entry point was also closely guarded against detection by the enemy, who could have also entered into the underground tunnels by this opening, and attempted a surprise attack.

These are some of the weapons employed in the Vietnam War. They vary from regular artillery to other makeshift weapons constructed by the local fighters.

This photo documents some of the victims in the
Vietnam conflict, and the tragic loss of life.

These pictures are part of the photo collection in the Vietnam War Museum, which document some of the victims in the Vietnam conflict, and the tragic loss of life.

A smaller museum in the local town also commemorates
the innocent victims of the Vietnam War.

Photos document the War in the Vietnam War Museum

A Tribute to the Victims at the Vietnam War Museum

This massive graveyard memorializes the Tragic Victims of the Vietnam War.

This statue in the Vietnam memorial shows a mother mourning the loss of her son in the Vietnam War.

This wall at the Vietnam Memorial honors the many victims of that conflict.

*The End*

Printed in the United States
by Baker & Taylor Publisher Services